To:

_____

From:

_____

And God said, "Let the water teem with living creatures, and let birds fly above the
earth across the expanse of the sky." So God created the great creatures of the sea and
every living and moving thing with which the water teems, according to their kinds,
and every winged bird according to its kind. And God saw that it was good.

Genesis 1:20-21

The Helen Steiner Rice Foundation

When someone does a kindness
It always seems to me
That's the way God up in heaven
Would like us all to be . . .

Whatever the celebration, whatever the day, whatever the event, whatever the occasion, Helen Steiner Rice possessed the ability to express the appropriate feeling for that particular moment in time. Her positive attitude, her concern for others, and her love of God are identifiable threads woven into her life, her work . . . and even her death.

Prior to Mrs. Rice's passing, she established the Helen Steiner Rice Foundation, a non-profit corporation that awards grants to worthy charitable programs assisting the elderly and the needy.

Royalties from the sale of this book will add to the financial capabilities of the Helen Steiner Rice Foundation. Because of limited resources, the foundation presently limits grants to qualified charitable programs in Lorain, Ohio, where Helen Steiner Rice was born and Greater Cincinnati, Ohio, where Mrs. Rice lived and worked most of her life. Hopefully in the future, resources will be of sufficient size that broader areas may be considered in the awarding of grants. Thank you for your assistance in helping to keep Helen's dream alive and growing.

ANDREA R. CORNETT, ADMINISTRATOR

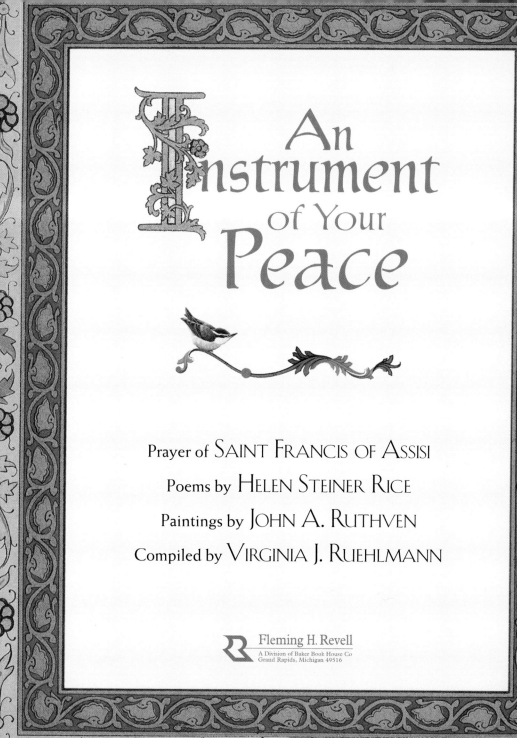

An Instrument of Your Peace

Prayer of SAINT FRANCIS OF ASSISI

Poems by HELEN STEINER RICE

Paintings by JOHN A. RUTHVEN

Compiled by VIRGINIA J. RUEHLMANN

Fleming H. Revell
A Division of Baker Book House Co
Grand Rapids, Michigan 49516

Published by Fleming H. Revell
a division of Baker Book House Company
P.O. Box 6287, Grand Rapids, MI 49516-6287

Printed in the United States of America

Library of Congress Cataloging-in-Publication Data

Rice, Helen Steiner.
    An instrument of your peace / poems by Helen Steiner Rice; paintings by John Ruthven; compiled by Virginia J. Ruehlmann.
       p.   cm.
    Includes the Prayer of Saint Francis of Assisi.
    ISBN 0-8007-1783-X
    1. Christian poetry, American. I. Ruthven, John A. II. Ruehlmann, Virginia J. III. Title.
    PS3568.I28 A6 2001
    811′.54—dc   2001031739

Jacket and interior designed by Robin K. Black.

For current information about all releases from Baker Book House, visit our web site:
http://www.bakerbooks.com

To all individuals who advocate and promote
a peaceful attitude and who practice in daily life
the virtues enumerated in the prayer of Saint Francis of Assisi

May the prayer of Saint Francis speak to us of hope and faith and love—
Hope to light our pathway when the way ahead is dark,
Hope to sing through stormy days with the sweetness of a lark,
Faith to trust in things unseen and know beyond all seeing
That it is in our Father's love we live and have our being,
And love to break down barriers of color, race and creed,
Love to see and understand and help all those in need.

HSR

I know every bird in the mountains, and the creatures of the field are mine. Psalm 50:11

The year 1182 was like our own times—torn by political, economic, and spiritual crises. Francis Bernardone was born that year in the small Italian town of Assisi. His parents were wealthy and indulgent, and he had a happy-go-lucky childhood and youth, filled with dreams of becoming a knight. But he went off to war and became disillusioned.

Little by little, however, Francis underwent a conversion and won peace and joy as he followed the example of Jesus, who "emptied himself." It was Francis' ability to love unconditionally that made him the "instrument of peace" that he was and the inspiration that he is.

An Instrument of Your Peace seizes upon the inspiration of Saint Francis of Assisi and his timeless message. His often cited *Peace Prayer* is easily woven into the inspirational words of Helen Steiner Rice, a poet with a Franciscan heart. Is it any wonder that the art of John Ruthven should find its way into a book inspired by Saint Francis? Ruthven nature scenes would have warmed the heart of Francis, who saw God's hand at work in all creation. The blending of Francis' words and John Ruthven's art is a perfect fit.

The words, the art, and the music of this book will sooth and calm you. May they also inspire you to know that joy and peace are possible.

Pax et Bonum.

FRIAR JAMES BOK, O.F.M.
SAINT FRANCIS SERAPH FRIARY
PROVINCE OF SAINT JOHN THE BAPTIST
CINCINNATI, OHIO

Prayer of Saint Francis of Assisi

Lord, make me an instrument of Your peace.
Where there is hatred, let me sow love,
Where there is injury, pardon,
Where there is doubt, faith,
Where there is despair, hope,
Where there is darkness, light,
And where there is sadness, joy.
O Divine Master, grant that I may not so much seek
To be consoled, as to console,
To be understood, as to understand,
To be loved, as to love.
For it is in giving that we receive,
It is in pardoning that we are pardoned,
And it is in dying that we are born to eternal life.

SAINT FRANCIS OF ASSISI

Channels of Blessing

Saint Francis' adherence to the principles of faith, hope, love, charity, forgiveness, consolation, understanding, and his endeavors to minimize hatred, injury, doubt, despair, darkness, sadness, set an example of selflessness for the world to emulate and a model to imitate. Saint Francis loved "all creatures of our God and King" and wrote the hymn emphasizing this fact.

The inspirational words and convictions of Helen Steiner Rice are appropriately interrelated with the equally encouraging and heartening ideology and doctrines stated by Saint Francis. Coupled with the incredibly accurate and detailed artwork of John Ruthven, who captures the precise expressions of God's wildlife in his nature paintings, the reader will profit from and enjoy the message and art in this book. More and more it is evident that animals and birds add essential qualities to our lives, our environment, our health, and our mental and emotional outlook.

Mrs. Rice's final years were spent as a resident of Mercy Franciscan Terrace in Cincinnati, Ohio, where in keeping with the name she was touched by gentle, helping hands and received encouraging words and spiritual strength. While a patient and restricted to bed rest an Honorary Degree of Doctor of Humane Letters was bestowed upon Helen Steiner Rice from the College of Mount Saint Joseph in March 1981. Thus Helen Steiner Rice realized a childhood goal of receiving a degree from college. It was not the undergraduate or law degree that she once had planned. She relinquished that objective when she became the family's breadwinner following her father's unexpected demise in 1917 and after her graduation from high school.

May this work assist you to continue in your efforts to be an instrument of peace, to find and sustain in your life the qualities of love, pardon, faith, forgiveness, and all the virtues espoused by Saint Francis, described in verse by Helen Steiner Rice, and depicted in art form by John Ruthven.

May His peace be with you,
Virginia J. Ruehlmann

Lord, make me an instrument of Your peace

The Peace We're Seeking

If we but had the eyes to see God's face in every cloud,
If we but had the ears to hear His voice above the crowd,
If we could feel His gentle touch in every springtime breeze
And find a haven in His arms 'neath sheltering, leafy trees.
If we could just lift up our hearts like flowers to the sun
And trust His loving promise and pray, "Thy will be done,"
We'd find the peace we're seeking, the kind no man can give—
The peace that comes from knowing He died so we might live!

Jesus said to them again, "Peace be with you. As the Father has sent me, even so I send you." John 20:21 RSV

Lift up your heart to permit God's message and promise to be revealed.

10

God Grants You the Peace You Seek

Beyond that which words can interpret or theology explain,
The soul feels a shower of refreshment that falls like the gentle rain
On hearts that are parched with problems and are searching to find the way
To somehow attract God's attention through well-chosen words as they pray,
Not knowing that God in His wisdom can sense all our worry and woe,
For there is nothing we can conceal that God does not already know.
So kneel in prayer in His presence and you'll find no need to speak,
For softly in quiet communion, God grants you the peace that you seek.

"Peace, peace, to the far and to the near, says the LORD; *and I will heal him."* Isaiah 57:19 RSV

Peace, like a gentle rain, can wash away tension and bestow a refreshing touch.

11

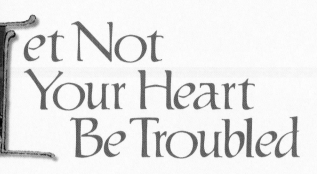

et Not Your Heart Be Troubled

Whenever I am troubled and lost in deep despair,
I bundle all my troubles up and go to God in prayer.
I tell Him I am heartsick and lost and lonely, too,
That my mind is deeply burdened and I don't know what to do.
I know He stilled the tempest and calmed the angry sea,
And I humbly ask if, in His love, He'll do the same for me.
And then I just keep quiet and think only thoughts of peace,
And if I abide in stillness my restless murmurings cease.

And he awoke and rebuked the wind, and said to the sea, "Peace! Be still!"
And the wind ceased, and there was a great calm. Mark 4:39 RSV

A sense of tranquility is attained with quiet time.

The Better You Know God the Better You'll Feel

The better you know God the better you'll feel,
For to learn more about Him and discover He's real
Can wholly, completely and miraculously change,
Reshape and remake and then rearrange
Your mixed-up, miserable and unhappy life
Adrift on the sea of sin-sickened strife.
But when you once know the Man of Good Will,
He will calm your life and say, "Peace, be still."
So open your heart's door and let Christ come in,
And He'll give you new life and free you from sin.
And there is no joy that can ever compare
With the joy of knowing that you're in God's care.

The doors were shut, but Jesus came and stood among them, and said,
"Peace be with you." John 20:26 RSV

Have you responded to His knock?

13

When Troubles Come and Things Go Wrong

Let us go quietly to God when troubles come to us.
Let us never stop to whimper or complain or fret or fuss.
Let us hide our thorns in roses and our sighs in golden song
And our crosses in a crown of smiles whenever things go wrong.
For no one can really help us as our troubles we bemoan,
For comfort, help and inner peace must come from God alone.
So do not tell your neighbor, your companion or your friend
In the hope that they can help you bring your troubles to an end,
For they too have their problems—they are burdened just like you—
So take your cross to Jesus, and He will see you through
And waste no time in crying on the shoulder of a friend,
But go directly to the Lord, for on Him you can depend.
For there's absolutely nothing that His mighty hand can't do,
And He never is too busy to help and comfort you.

"Hear my prayer, O LORD, and give ear to my cry; hold not thy peace at my tears!" Psalm 39:12 RSV

Your Lord is always available to listen to you.

14

here there
is hatred,
let me
sow love

What Is Love?

What is love? No words can define it—
It's something so great only God could design it.
Wonder of wonders, beyond our conception—
And only in God can love find true perfection.
Yes, love is beyond what we can define,
For love is immortal and God's gift is divine.

He who does not love does not know God; for God is love. 1 John 4:8 RSV

God is the greatest source of love. Be true to your Savior and yourself and love will radiate from within.

Those We Love

Often through the passing days we feel deep down inside
Unspoken thoughts of thankfulness and fond, admiring pride—
Words can say so little when the heart is overflowing,
And often those we love the most just have no way of knowing
The many things the heart conceals and never can impart
For words seem so inadequate to express what's in the heart.

Little children, let us not love in word or speech but in deed and in truth. 1 John 3:18 RSV

When departing from loved ones, even for a brief time, be sure to say "I love you."

17

God of Love

God of love, forgive—forgive. Teach us how to truly live.
Ask not our race or creed, just take us in our hour of need
And let us know You love us, too, and that we are a part of You.
And someday may we realize that all the earth, the seas and skies
Belong to God, who made us all—the rich, the poor, the great, the small—
In the Father's holy sight no one is yellow, black or white.
And peace on earth cannot be found until we meet on common ground
And every one becomes a sister or brother who worships God and loves each other.

*"You have heard that it was said, 'You shall love your neighbor and hate your enemy.' But I say to you,
Love your enemies and pray for those who persecute you."* Matthew 5:43-44 RSV

Let your life be a model of agape love.

18

Love

Love is enduring and patient and kind—
It judges all things with the heart, not the mind . . .
And love can transform the most commonplace
Into beauty and splendor and sweetness and grace.
For love is unselfish—giving more than it takes—
And no matter what happens, love never forsakes.
It's faithful and trusting and always believing,
Guileless and honest and never deceiving.

Love bears all things, believes all things, hopes all things, endures all things. 1 Corinthians 13:7 RSV

Love is constant, kind, and unwavering.

To My Love

In my eyes there lies no vision but the sight of your dear face;
In my heart there is no feeling but the warmth of your embrace.
In my mind there are no thoughts but the thoughts of you, my dear;
In my soul no other longing but just to have you near.
All my dreams are built around you and I've come to know it's true,
In my life there is no living that is not a part of you.

If we love one another, God abides in us and his love is perfected in us. 1 John 4:12 RSV

God is the greatest source of love. Confide in Him, pray to Him, trust in Him, and love Him.

here there is
injury,
pardon

ore of Thee— Less of Me

Take me and break me and make me, dear God, just what You want me to be.
Give me the strength to accept what You send and eyes with the vision to see
All the small, arrogant ways that I have and the vain little things that I do.
Make me aware that I'm often concerned more with myself than with You.
Uncover before me my weakness and greed and help me to search deep inside
So I may discover how easy it is to be selfishly lost in my pride.
And then in Thy goodness and mercy, look down on this weak, erring one
And tell me that I am forgiven for all I've so willfully done,
And teach me to humbly start following the path that the dear Savior trod
So I'll find at the end of life's journey a home in the city of God.

*"Judge not, and you will not be judged; condemn not, and you will not be condemned; forgive,
and you will be forgiven." Luke 6:37 RSV*

Recognize not only the spiritual value of forgiveness but also the therapeutic benefits.

God's Forgiveness

Each day at dawning we have but to pray
    that all the mistakes that we made yesterday
Will be blotted out and forgiven by grace,
    for God, in His mercy, will completely efface
All that is past, and He'll grant a new start
    to all who are truly repentant at heart,
And well may we pause in awesome-like wonder,
    that our Father in heaven, who dwells far asunder,
Could still remain willing to freely forgive
    the shabby, small lives we so selfishly live;
But this is the gift of God's limitless love,
    a gift that we all are so unworthy of.

"The time has come," he said. "The kingdom of God is near. Repent and believe the good news!" Mark 1:15

Is your reflection one of sincere forgiveness?

To Really Live Is to Give and Forgive

Since God forgives us, we too must forgive
And resolve to do better each day that we live
By constantly trying to be like Him more nearly
And to trust in His wisdom and to love Him more dearly.

Bear with each other and forgive whatever grievances you may have against one another. Forgive as the Lord forgave you.
Colossians 3:13

God offers a second chance to us; let us do no less to those who offend us.

24

here there
is doubt,
faith

aith to Climb Till Your Dream Comes True

Often your tasks will be many, and more than you think you can do.
Often the road will be rugged, and the hills insurmountable, too.
But always remember, the hills ahead are never as steep as they seem,
And with faith in your heart, start upward and climb till you reach
your dream.

For nothing in life that is worthy is ever too hard to achieve
If you have the courage to try it and you have the faith to believe.
For faith is a force that is greater than knowledge or power or skill,
And many defeats turn to triumphs if you trust in God's wisdom and will.
For faith is a mover of mountains—there's nothing that God cannot do—
So start out today with faith in your heart and climb till your dream comes true.

No temptation has seized you except what is common to man. And God is faithful; he will not let you be tempted
beyond what you can bear. But when you are tempted, he will also provide a way out so that you can stand up under it.
1 Corinthians 10:13

No mountain is too high, no task impossible, no dream unattainable with faith in your heart and trust in God.

Faith as a Grain of Mustard Seed

When the way seems long and the day is dark
   and we can't hear the sound of the thrush or the lark
And our hearts are heavy with worry and care
   and we are lost in the depths of despair,
That is the time when faith alone
   can lead us out of the dark unknown.

For faith to believe when the way is rough
    and faith to hang on when the going is tough
Will never fail to pull us through
    and bring us strength and comfort, too.
For all we really ever need
    is faith as a grain of mustard seed,
For all God asks is do you believe—
    for if you do you shall receive.

"For truly, I say to you, if you have faith as a grain of mustard seed, you will say to this mountain 'Move from here to there,'
and it will move; and nothing will be impossible to you." Matthew 17:20 RSV

Do you believe? If you do, you will receive!

The Dawning

The sun just rising in the sky as night is tucked away,
The joy of just awakening to a new and untouched day,
The beauty of the dawning, the freshness of the dew,
The inky clouds of darkness becoming azure blue
Are daily little miracles that speak of God's great glory—
For who can watch the dawning and doubt the Easter story?

"Have faith in God," Jesus answered. Mark 11:22

Help me to appreciate completely the strength, the meaning, and the significance of Easter.

Security and Encouragement

To know beyond belief that Someone cares
and hears our prayers
provides security for the soul, peace of mind
and joy of heart
that no earthly trials, tribulations, sickness or sorrow can penetrate.
For faith makes it wholly possible to quietly endure
the violent world around us, for in God we are secure.

Your kingdom is an everlasting kingdom, and your dominion endures through all generations.
The LORD is faithful to all his promises and loving toward all he has made. Psalm 145:13

God covers us with a security blanket of faith. Take advantage of its warmth.

ive by Faith and Not by Feelings

When everything is pleasant and bright
   and the things we do turn out just right,
We feel without question that God is real,
   for when we are happy, how good we feel.
But when the tides turn and gone is the song
   and misfortune comes and our plans go wrong,
Doubt creeps in and we start to wonder
   and our thoughts about God are torn asunder—
And it is when our senses are reeling
   we realize clearly it's faith and not feeling,
For it takes great faith to patiently wait,
   believing God comes not too soon or too late.

Commit your way to the LORD; trust in him and he will do this: He will make your righteousness shine like the dawn,
the justice of your cause like the noonday sun. Psalm 37:5-6

May your faith be fervent despite the weather, surroundings, or circumstances.

here
there is
despair,
hope

I Come to Meet You

I come to meet You, God, and as I linger here I seem to feel You very near.
A rustling leaf, a rolling slope, speak to my heart of endless hope.
The sun just rising in the sky, the waking birdlings as they fly,
The grass all wet with morning dew are telling me I just met You
And, gently, thus the day is born as night gives way to breaking morn,
And once again I've met You, God, and worshipped on Your holy sod.
For who could see the dawn break through without a glimpse of heaven and You?
For who but God could make the day and softly put the night away?

"And you will have confidence, because there is hope; you will be protected and take your rest in safety." Job 11:18 RSV

From morning to night maintain a high level of hope, confident that God will take care of you.

Wings of Prayer and Love

Meet God in the morning and go with Him through the day,
And thank Him for His guidance each evening when you pray—
And if you follow faithfully this daily way to pray,
You will never in your lifetime face another hopeless day.
For, like a soaring eagle, you too can rise above
The storms of life around you on the wings of prayer and love.

"And now, Lord, for what do I wait? My hope is in thee." Psalm 39:7 RSV

Daily prayers and love will sustain you and carry you through the turbulent times of life.

Not What You Want but What God Wills

Do you want what you want when you want it? Do you pray and expect a reply?
And when it's not instantly answered, do you feel that God passed you by?
Well, prayers that are prayed in this manner are really not prayers at all,
For you can't go to God in a hurry and expect Him to answer your call.
For prayers are not meant for obtaining what we selfishly wish to acquire,
For God in His wisdom refuses the things that we wrongly desire.

And don't pray for freedom from trouble or pray that life's trials pass you by,
Instead pray for strength and for courage to meet life's dark hours and not cry
That God was not there when you called Him and He turned a deaf ear to your prayer
And just when you needed Him most of all He left you alone in despair.
Wake up! You are missing completely the reason and purpose of prayer,
Which is really to keep us contented that God holds us safe in His care.
And God only answers our pleadings when He knows that our wants fill a need,
And whenever our will becomes His will there is no prayer that God does not heed.

I trust in God's unfailing love forever and ever. I will praise you forever for what you have done; in your name I will hope, for your name is good. I will praise you in the presence of your saints. Psalm 52:8-9

Know that God always hears your prayer. Be patient in waiting for the answer.

The Great Tomorrow

There is always a tomorrow. Tomorrow belongs as much to you as it does to me.
The dawn of a new day means the dawn of a new life.
We cannot peer into its storehouse, but the very impenetrable mystery
which enwraps the ever-approaching tomorrow
is the one thing that keeps the fires of hope constantly burning.
No matter what our yesterdays have been, tomorrow may be different.
As long as we have life, the fires of hope will not die out; the flame may burn low,
but at the thought of a new day, the flame which seemed dead leaps forward
and the sparks once more fly upward to spur us on.

"Therefore do not be anxious about tomorrow, for tomorrow will be anxious for itself.
Let the day's own trouble be sufficient for the day." Matthew 6:34 RSV

Face the troubles of today with optimism, knowing that after twenty-four hours today will become
yesterday, and tomorrow will appear as today with fresh opportunities.

38

It's Me Again, God

Remember me, God? I come every day
Just to talk with You, Lord, and to learn how to pray.
You make me feel welcome, You reach out Your hand.
I need never explain, for You understand.
I come to You frightened and burdened with care,
So lonely and lost and so filled with despair,
And suddenly, Lord, I'm no longer afraid—
My burden is lighter and the dark shadows fade.
Oh God, what a comfort to know that You care
And to know when I seek You, You will always be there.

*"For I know the plans I have for you, says the LORD, plans for welfare and not for evil,
to give you a future and a hope." Jeremiah 29:11 RSV*

Thank you, God, for being available and willing to listen to me.

Words to Live By

We all need words to live by to inspire us and to guide us,
Words to give us courage when the trials of life betide us.
And the words that never fail us are the words of God above,
Words of comfort and of courage filled with wisdom and with love.
They are ageless and enduring, they have lived through generations—
There's no question left unanswered in our Father's revelations.
And in this ever-changing world God's words remain unchanged,
For though through countless ages they've been often rearranged,
The truth shines through all changes just as bright today as when
Our Father made the universe and breathed His life in men.

So whenever you are troubled and your heart is sad with sorrow,
You'll find comfort, strength and courage to help you meet tomorrow
If you will cast your burden completely on the Lord,
For faith that does not falter will bring its own reward.
And through the darkest hours of deep discouragement,
God is your strength and refuge and your soul's encouragement.

"But the word of the Lord abides for ever." That word is the good news which was preached to you. 1 Peter 1:25 RSV

The power of Your good news encourages me.

Silver Lining

When trouble comes as it does to us all,
We feel so helpless and lost and small—
Our world falls apart, and in despair
We see no beauty anywhere.
But behind the clouds the sun is shining,
For every cloud has a silver lining.

"I have set my rainbow in the clouds, and it will be the sign of the covenant between me and the earth." Genesis 9:13

Some days I cannot see the rainbow or the silver lining. Please improve my vision and my hope.

42

Where there is darkness, light

Light

God made the sun, He made the sky,
He made the trees, and the birds that fly.
God made the flowers, He made the light,
He made the stars that shine at night.

And God said, "Let there be light," and there was light. Genesis 1:3

Dear God, thank You for turning the night into day, winter into spring,
sadness into gladness, and death into eternal life.

44

I Am Light

Each time you look up in the sky
Or watch a fluffy cloud go by
Or feel the sunshine warm and bright
Or watch the dark night turn to light
Or hear a bluebird gayly sing
Or see the winter turn to spring
Or stop to pick a daffodil
Or gather violets on some hill
Or touch a leaf or see a tree—
It's all God whispering, "This is me,
And I am faith and I am light
And in Me there shall be no night."

"You are my lamp, O LORD; the LORD turns my darkness into light." 2 Samuel 22:29

Each ray of sunshine beams a message from God.

The Eternal Light

The Lord is our salvation
And our strength in every fight,
Our redeemer and protector,
Our eternal guiding light.
He has promised to sustain us,
He's our refuge from all harms,
And He holds us all securely
In His everlasting arms!

The Lord is my light and my salvation—whom shall I fear? Psalm 27:1

Thank You for illuminating my life.

A Brighter Day

In sickness or health, in suffering and pain,
In storm-laden skies, in sunshine and rain,
God always is there to lighten your way
And lead you through darkness to a much brighter day.

*God saw that the light was good, and he separated the light from the darkness. God called the light "day,"
and the darkness he called "night." Genesis 1:4-5*

Permit me to be a conductor of light.

Love Lights the Path

We stumble in darkness groping vainly for light
To distinguish the difference between wrong and right.
But dawn cannot follow this night of despair
Unless faith lights a candle in all hearts everywhere.
And, warmed by the glow, our hate melts away
And love lights the path to a peaceful new day.

Your word is a lamp to my feet and a light for my path. Psalm 119:105

Help me to light the pathway in someone's life.

And where
there is
sadness,
joy

ake Nothing for Granted

Take nothing for granted for whenever you do,
The joy of enjoying is lessened for you.
We rob our own lives much more than we know
When we fail to respond or in any way show
Our thanks for the blessings that daily are ours—
The warmth of the sun, the fragrance of flowers,
The beauty of twilight, the freshness of dawn,
The coolness of dew on a green velvet lawn,
The kind little deeds so thoughtfully done,
The favors of friends and the love that someone
Unselfishly gives us in a myriad of ways,
Expecting no payment and no words of praise.

Great is our loss when we no longer find
A thankful response to things of this kind.
For the joy of enjoying and the fullness of living
Are found in the heart filled with thanks giving.

Be joyful always. 1 Thessalonians 5:16

Joy is a tonic for the heart. It makes a sunny day sunnier, a lovely memory lovelier.

Expectation! Anticipation! Realization!

God gives us a power we so seldom employ
For we're so unaware it is filled with such joy,
The gift that God gives us is anticipation,
Which we can fulfill with sincere expectation,
For there's power in belief when we think we will find
Joy for the heart and peace for the mind,
And believing the day will bring a surprise
Is not only pleasant but surprisingly wise.
For we open the door to let joy walk through
When we learn to expect the best and most, too,
And believing we'll find a happy surprise
Makes reality out of a fancied surmise.

"If you keep my commandments, you will abide in my love, just as I have kept my Father's commandments and abide in his love. These things I have spoken to you, that my joy may be in you, and that your joy may be full." John 15:10-11 RSV

Father, help me to look forward to each day with great anticipation
and inspire me to bring joy into the life of another individual.

52

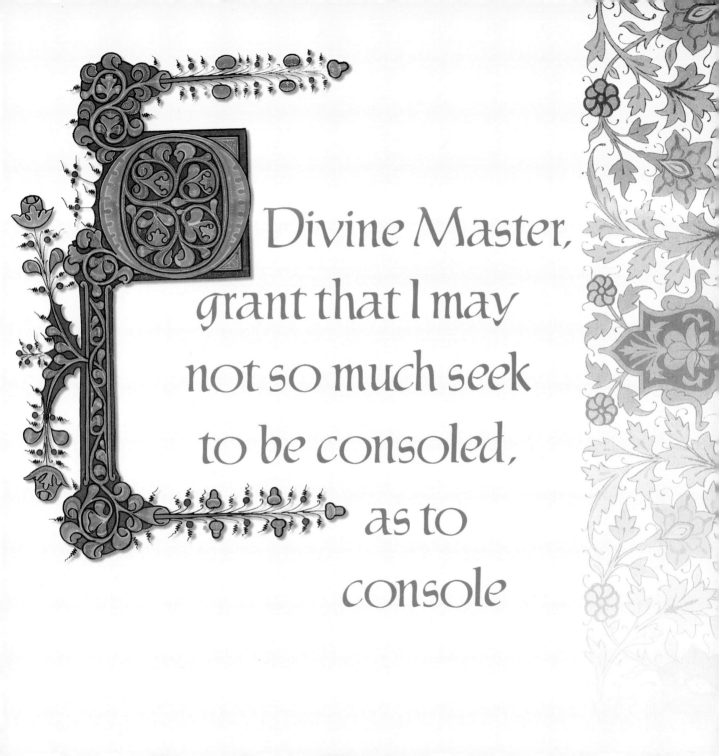

Divine Master, grant that I may not so much seek to be consoled, as to console

Message of Consolation

On the wings of death and sorrow
God sends us new hope for tomorrow,
And in His mercy and His grace
He gives us strength to bravely face
The lonely days that stretch ahead
And to know our loved one is not dead
But only sleeping out of our sight,
And we'll meet in that land where there is no night.

The LORD is my shepherd, I shall not want; he makes me lie down in green pastures.
He leads me beside still waters; he restores my soul. Psalm 23:1-3 RSV

Visualize the miraculous transformation of a bulb buried in the earth into a blooming, fragrant lily.

God's Presence

Whenever you are troubled
　　may you feel God's presence near.
May the greatness of His mercy
　　and the sweetness of His peace
Bring you everlasting comfort
　　and the joys that never cease.

When anxiety was great within me, your consolation brought joy to my soul. Psalm 94:19

Knowing God is ever present should be a source of comfort and tranquility for you.

55

A New Sense of God

I find that all that was once possible for me to do with joyful eagerness
and bubbling enthusiasm has somehow become more difficult.
These days I find that the greatest source of comfort
and inner peace and the only thing that can lift us above our earthly bondage
is the deep sense of aloneness with God—which is not loneliness—
for we only find true spiritual communion when we are alone
and can have direct communication with God.

May your unfailing love be my comfort, according to your promise to your servant. Psalm 119:76

Spend even a few minutes in meditation with God and you gain hours of peace and solace.

Help for Each Day

It makes me sad to think of you so filled with pain and discomfort, too,
And I know there's nothing I can do but talk to the Lord and pray for you.
I wish I could wipe away every trace of pain and suffering from your face,
But He is great and we are small—we just can't alter His will at all—
And none of us would want to try, for more and more as days go by
We know His plan for us is best and He will give us peace and rest.
And earthly pain is never too much if He has bestowed His merciful touch,
And if you will look to Him and pray, He will help you through every day.

"As I was with Moses, so I will be with you; I will never leave you nor forsake you." Joshua 1:5

As you sustain someone in their time of adversity, your own troubles are forgotten.

To Heal and Comfort You

I wish I knew some magic words to say to take your troubles all away.
But at times like this we realize that God Who is both kind and wise
Can do what none of us can do and that's to heal and comfort you.
So I commend you to His care, and may God hear your smallest prayer
And grant returning health to you as only God alone can do.

Blessed be the God and Father of our Lord Jesus Christ, the Father of mercies and God of all comfort,
who comforts us in all our affliction, so that we may be able to comfort those who are in any affliction,
with the comfort with which we ourselves are comforted by God. 2 Corinthians 1:3-4 RSV

Assist others to maintain their dignity at all times.

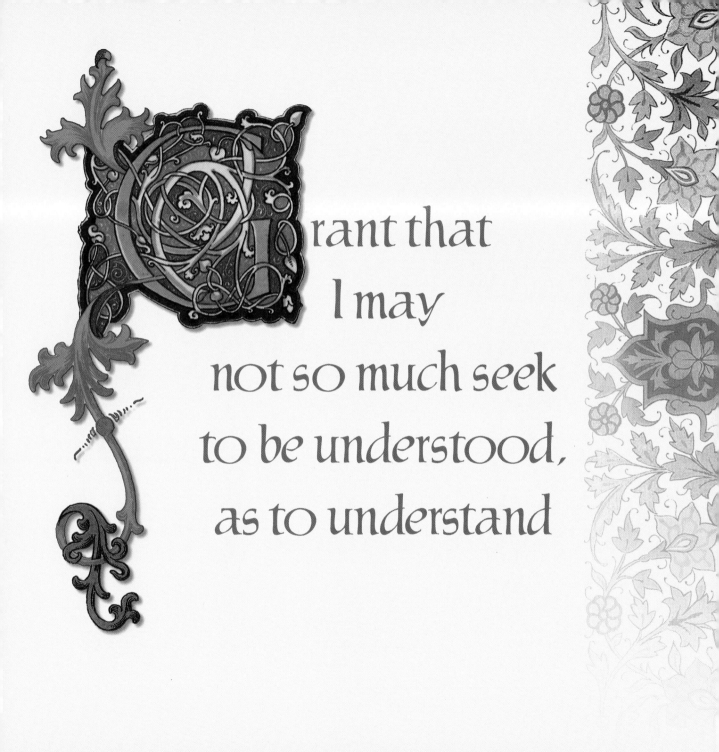

Grant that
I may
not so much seek
to be understood,
as to understand

You Are in His Care

While we cannot understand why things happen as they do,
The Man who hangs the rainbow out has His own plans for you.
And when the dark days come and we cannot understand,
We must trust God's wisdom and be guided by His hand.
And may it comfort you to know that you are in His care,
For we are all a part of God and God is everywhere.

Trust in the LORD with all your heart and lean not on your own understanding. Proverbs 3:5

Trust in God as Saint Francis did.

Help Us to See and Understand

God, give us wider vision to see and understand
That both the sunshine and the showers are gifts from Thy great hand.
And when our lives are overcast with trouble and with care,
Give us faith to see beyond the dark clouds of despair.
And give us strength to rise above the mist of doubt and fear,
And recognize the hidden smile behind each burning tear.

My purpose is that they may be encouraged in heart and united in love, so that they may have
the full riches of complete understanding, in order that they may know the mystery of God, namely Christ,
in whom are hidden all the treasures of wisdom and knowledge. Colossians 2:2-3

Display your wisdom by practicing proper timing. Know when to speak a word of encouragement
and when an embrace extended silently is in order.

Listen

To try to run away from life is impossible to do,
For no matter where you chance to go, your troubles will follow you.
For though the scenery is different, when you look deep inside you'll find
The same deep restless longings that you thought you left behind.
So when life becomes a problem much too great for us to bear,
Instead of trying to escape, let us withdraw in prayer—
For withdrawal means renewal, if we withdraw to pray
And listen in the quietness to hear what God will say.

*And the peace of God, which transcends all understanding, will guard your hearts and
your minds in Christ Jesus. Philippians 4:7*

Renew your efforts to listen and to pray and you will be blessed with a spiritual renewal.

Higher View

God, give me strength for my stumbling feet
    as I battle the crowd on life's busy street.
And widen the vision of my unseeing eyes,
    so in passing faces, I'll recognize
Not just a stranger, unloved and unknown,
    but a friend with a heart much like my own.
Give me perception to make me aware
    that scattered profusely on life's thoroughfare
Are the best gifts of God that we daily pass by
    as we look at the world with an unseeing eye.

The scribe said to him: "Excellent, Teacher! You are right in saying, 'He is the One, there is no other than he.'
Yes, 'to love him with all our heart, with all our thoughts and with all our strength, and to love our neighbor
as ourselves' is worth more than any burnt offering or sacrifice." Mark 12:32-33 NAB

Focus on encouraging those around you. Be tireless in your efforts to inspire and motivate in a gentle and
tender manner, maintaining a warmth in your actions, generated by a sincere sense of understanding.

Understanding

Added years bring new dimensions
That enable us to see
All things within a kinder light
And more perceptively—
So each year becomes a gateway
To what the future holds
And to greater understanding
As the story of life unfolds.

Make me understand the way of thy precepts, and I will meditate on thy wondrous works. Psalm 119:27 RSV

Put yourself in the other person's place. Is that individual lonely? Offer companionship.
Is there a problem? Help to solve it. Is there a need of a prayer? Pray together.

Grant that
I may
not so much seek
to be loved
as to love

Where There Is Love

Where there is love the heart is light,
Where there is love the day is bright.
Where there is love there is a song
To help when things are going wrong.
Where there is love there is a smile
To make all things seem more worthwhile.

Where there is love there's a quiet peace,
A tranquil place where turmoils cease.
Love changes darkness into light
And makes the heart take wingless flight.
Oh, blessed are those who walk in love—
They also walk with God above.

And walk in love, as Christ loved us and gave himself up for us,
a fragrant offering and sacrifice to God. Ephesians 5:2 RSV

Love is a heavenly gift bequeathed by God.

Lasting Love

A lasting love is made of sharing
A happy home that's filled with caring.
It's made of planning and dreaming together,
Facing with courage life's stormiest weather.
And nothing on earth or in heaven can part
Two people whose love grows deep in the heart.

Love does not insist on its own way; it is not irritable or resentful; it does not rejoice at wrong,
but rejoices in the right. 1 Corinthians 13:5-6 RSV

Persevere in maintaining a loving relationship. There is always more energy
and another ounce of love within you.

World of Love

To speak, to act, to work with love
    is something we know little of—
Love that transcends all comprehension
    and knows no limit or dimension.
Love that is bigger than the land
    and much too great to understand,
Love reaching to the world's far ends
    transforming strangers into friends.
What greater gift could anyone bring
    than love that touches everything,
A love so meaningful and wide,
    the whole wide world is wrapped inside.

Make love your aim, and earnestly desire the spiritual gifts. 1 Corinthians 14:1 RSV

Words and time are not like yo-yos. Once a word is spoken it can never be retracted.
Once a minute is lost it cannot be found again. Value and safeguard both.

Friends Need Friends

People need people and friends need friends
And we all need love, for a full life depends
Not on vast riches or great acclaim,
Not on success or worldly fame,
But on just knowing that someone cares
And holds us close in their thoughts and prayers.
For only the knowledge that we're understood
Makes everyday living feel wonderfully good.

And we rob ourselves of life's greatest need
When we lock up our hearts and fail to heed
The outstretched hand reaching to find
A kindred spirit whose heart and mind
Are lonely and longing to somehow share
Our joys and sorrows and to make us aware
That life's completeness and richness depend
On the things we share with our loved ones and friends.

Above all hold unfailing your love for one another. 1 Peter 4:8 RSV

Hold fast to and protect those closest to your heart.

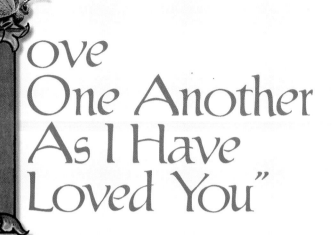

"Love One Another As I Have Loved You"

To love one another as God loved you
   may seem impossible to do,
But if you will try to have faith and believe,
   there's no end to the joy that you will receive.
For love works in ways that are wondrous and strange,
   and there's nothing in life that love cannot change—
For love is the key that throws open the door
   to the heart that was locked and lonely before.
Love is the answer to all the heart seeks,
   and love is the channel through which God speaks—
And all He has promised can only come true
   when you love one another the way He loved you.

I give you a new commandment: / Love one another. / Such as my love has been for you, / so must your love be for each other.
John 13:34 NAB

A kind word or thoughtful action is always appreciated.

Remembrance Road

There's a road I call remembrance where I walk each day with you;
It's a pleasant, happy road all filled with memories true.
Today it leads me through a spot where I can dream a while,
And in its tranquil peacefulness I touch your hand and smile.
There are hills and fields and budding trees and stillness that's so sweet,
That it seems that this must be the place where God and humans meet.
I hope we can go back again and golden hours renew,
And may God go with you always, until the day we do.

Dear friends, let us love one another. 1John 4:7

Enjoy your fond memories. Recalling those you love is good for you.

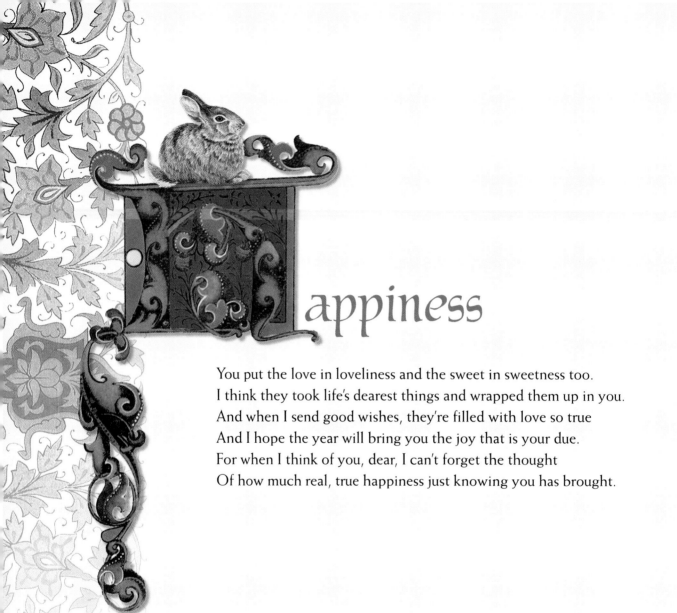

Happiness

You put the love in loveliness and the sweet in sweetness too.
I think they took life's dearest things and wrapped them up in you.
And when I send good wishes, they're filled with love so true
And I hope the year will bring you the joy that is your due.
For when I think of you, dear, I can't forget the thought
Of how much real, true happiness just knowing you has brought.

Whatever is lovely, whatever is admirable—if anything is excellent or praiseworthy,
think about such things. Philippians 4:8

Happiness adds to your tranquility.

It is
in giving
that
we receive

Not in Getting but in Giving

Only what we give away
    enriches us from day to day,
For not in getting but in giving
    is found the lasting joy of living.
For no one ever had a part
    in sharing treasures of the heart
Who did not feel the impact of
    the magic mystery of God's love.
And love alone can make us kind
    and give us joy and peace of mind,
So live with joy unselfishly
    and you'll be blessed abundantly.

"If your enemy is hungry, feed him; if he is thirsty, give him something to drink." Romans 12:20

Caring and sharing go hand in hand.

76

Happiness Given Away Returns to You

Everybody everywhere seeks happiness, it's true,
But finding it and keeping it seem difficult to do—
Difficult because we think that happiness is found
Only in the places where wealth and fame abound.
And so we go on searching in palaces of pleasure,
Seeking recognition and monetary treasure,
Unaware that happiness is just a state of mind
Within the reach of everyone who takes time to be kind.
For in making others happy, you will be happy, too,
For the happiness you give away returns to shine on you.

A happy heart makes the face cheerful. Proverbs 15:13

The way to increase your happiness is to share it with others.

Giving Is the Key to Living

Every day is a reason for giving
And giving is the key to living,
So let us give ourselves away,
Not just today but every day,
And remember, a kind and thoughtful deed
Or a hand outstretched in a time of need
Is the rarest of gifts, for it is a part
Not of the purse but a loving heart.
And he who gives of himself will find
True joy of heart and peace of mind.

Give, and it will be given to you. Luke 6:38

Like the traveling power of ripples in a lake, one act of kindness initiates a series
of peaceful waves in the river of life.

Teach Me to Share

Teach me to give of myself
in whatever way I can,
of whatever I have to give.
Teach me to value myself—
my time, my talents,
my purpose, my life,
my meaning in Your world.

"His Master replied, 'Well done, good and faithful servant! You have been faithful with a few things; I will put you in charge of many things. Come and share your master's happiness!'" Matthew 25:21

The wealth one has amassed is not as important as the good deeds accomplished
in life and the degree of love within the heart.

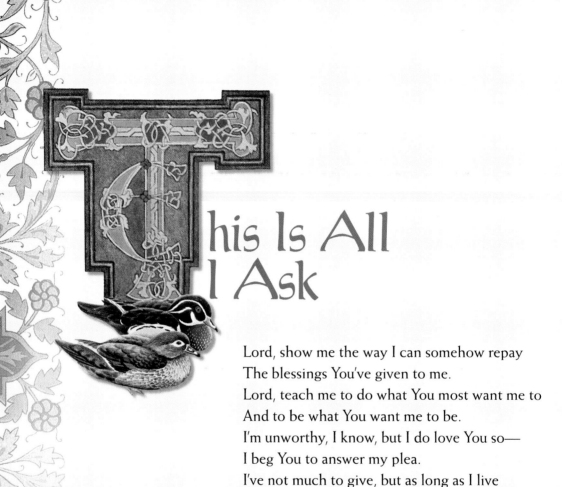

This Is All I Ask

Lord, show me the way I can somehow repay
The blessings You've given to me.
Lord, teach me to do what You most want me to
And to be what You want me to be.
I'm unworthy, I know, but I do love You so—
I beg You to answer my plea.
I've not much to give, but as long as I live
May I give it completely to Thee.

Share with God's people who are in need. Practice hospitality. Romans 12:13

God has given to each one the gift of originality and individuality. Avoid comparing yourself to others.
Each life is unique and each has a particular role to play.

It is
in pardoning
that *we*
are pardoned

Good Morning, God!

You are ushering in another day, untouched and freshly new,
So here I am to ask you, God, if You'll renew me, too.
Forgive the many errors that I made yesterday
And let me try again, dear God, to walk closer in Thy way.
But, Father, I am well aware I can't make it on my own,
So take my hand and hold it tight, for I cannot walk alone.

For thy name's sake, O LORD, pardon my guilt, for it is great. Psalm 25:11 RSV

Help me to overlook the unkind words said about me and the heartless actions directed toward me.

e All Make Mistakes

We all make mistakes—it's human to err—
But no one need ever give up in despair,
For God gives us all a brand-new beginning,
A chance to start over and repent of our sinning.
And when God forgives us, we too must forgive
And resolve to do better each day that we live
By constantly trying to be like Him more nearly
And to trust in His wisdom and to love Him more dearly—
Assured that we're never out of His care
And we're always welcome to seek Him in prayer.

I tell you that in the same way there will be more rejoicing in heaven over one sinner who repents than over ninety-nine righteous persons who do not need to repent. Luke 15:7

Advance forgiveness to enhance the quality of life.

Reassurance

Christ came and dwelled among us
and He knows our every need,
And He loves and understands us
and forgives each sinful deed.
So with this reassurance
may we meet the coming year
And find comfort, strength and courage
just in knowing He walked here.

When you stand to pray, forgive anyone against whom you have a grievance
so that your heavenly Father may in turn forgive you your faults. Mark 11:25 NAB

Demonstrate courage, strength, and the capacity to forgive in your everyday actions.
It's possible when you keep Christ as your example.

nd it is in dying that we are born to eternal life

Life Eternal

Somewhere there is a life eternal,
Somewhere there is a home above—
There is no night without a dawning,
Beyond this death is God and love.

And this is the testimony: God has given us eternal life, and this life is in his Son. He who has the Son has life;
he who does not have the Son of God does not have life. I write these things to you who believe in the name of the Son of God
so that you may know that you have eternal life. 1 John 5:11-13

When you extend sincere consolation to another, you yourself receive comfort.

The Gift of Eternal Life

With our eyes we see the beauty of Easter
   as the earth awakens once more.
With our ears we hear the birds sing sweetly
   to tell us spring again is here.
With our hands we pick the golden daffodils
   and the fragrant hyacinths.
But only with our hearts can we feel the miracle of God's love,
   which redeems us all—
And only with our souls can we make the pilgrimage to God
   and inherit His Easter gift of eternal life.

"The Father loves the Son and has placed everything in his hands. Whoever believes in the Son has eternal life, but whoever rejects the Son will not see life, for God's wrath remains on him." John 3:35-36

Our hands, eyes, and ears recognize the beauty of the Easter season;
our hearts discover God's love; and our souls perceive the value of eternal life.

87

All Nature Proclaims Eternal Life

Flowers sleeping beneath the snow,
Awakening when the spring winds blow,
Leafless trees so bare before
Gowned in lacy green once more,
Hard, unyielding, frozen sod
Now softly carpeted by God,
Still streams melting in the spring
Rippling over rocks that sing,
Barren, windswept, lonely hills
Turning gold with daffodils—

These miracles are all around
Within our sight and touch and sound,
As true and wonderful today
As when the stone was rolled away,
Proclaiming to all doubting women and men
That in God all things live again.

And they asked each other, "Who will roll the stone away from the entrance of the tomb?" But when they looked up, they saw that the stone, which was very large, had been rolled away. As they entered the tomb, they saw a young man dressed in a white robe sitting on the right side, and they were alarmed. Mark 16:3-5

Plant the seeds of faith with others and watch your own faith blossom, grow, and mature.

Why Should He Die for Such as I?

In everything both great and small we see the hand of God in all,
And in the miracle of spring, when everywhere in everything
His handiwork is all around and every lovely sight and sound
Proclaims the God of earth and sky, I ask myself—just who am I,
That God should send His only Son that my salvation would be won
Upon a cross by a sinless man to bring fulfillment to God's plan.
For Jesus suffered, bled and died that sinners might be sanctified
And to grant God's children such as I eternal life in that home on high.

Jesus said to her, "I am the resurrection and the life. He who believes in me will live, even though he dies;
and whoever lives and believes in me will never die. Do you believe this?" John 11:25-26

God's handiwork and His hand are always available to you.

The Gift of His Love

What better time and what better season,
What greater occasion or more wonderful reason
To kneel down in prayer and thank God above
For eternal life, the gift of His love.
For in sending His Son to be crucified,
He granted us life because His Son died.

*For God so loved the world that he gave his only Son, that whoever believes in him
should not perish but have eternal life. John 3:16 RSV*

Nature, the seasons, the flowers, even the butterfly tell us the story of death and resurrection.

Into a Brighter Day

There is no night without a dawning, no winter without a spring,
And beyond death's dark horizon our hearts once more will sing.
For those who leave us for a while have only gone away
Out of a restless, careworn world into a brighter day
Where there will be no partings and time is not counted by years—
Where there are no trials or troubles, no worries, no cares and no tears.

Eternal life is this: / to know you, the only true God, / and him whom you have sent, Jesus Christ. John 17:3 NAB

Our loved ones live on in our memories of times together, favorite songs, and happy happenings.

Bright New World

We feel so sad when those we love
  are touched by Death's dark hand,
But it would ease our sorrow
  if we could but understand
That death is just a gateway
  that all men and women must pass through,
And on the other side of death,
  in a world that's bright and new,
Our loved ones wait to welcome us
  to that land free from all tears
Where joy becomes eternal
  and time is not counted by years.

*"Truly, truly, I say to you, he who hears my word and believes him who sent me, has eternal life;
he does not come into judgment, but has passed from death to life."* John 5:24 RSV

Death is the opening to a new life with God and our loved ones in God's heavenly dwelling.

Life as a Peacemaker

Let us only compete
In giving instead of getting
In working for spiritual riches instead of material possessions
In acquiring virtue, instead of vice
In being good, instead of being great.

HSR

Live your life according to the principles found in the prayer of Saint Francis
and you will possess contentment, self-respect, love, and the ability
to encourage, forgive, and inspire others.

Balance your life by allotting time for
praying, meditating, thanking God for your blessings,
sharing time and feelings with family and friends,
singing, laughing, relaxing,
never being so busy
that you refuse the opportunity
to listen to another individual—adult or child,
acting as a peacemaker,
sowing love,
forgiving, pardoning,
spreading hope,
enlightening,
radiating joy,
encouraging, consoling, reaching out to someone,
understanding, loving, giving,
and believing in eternal life.

                                        VJR

Acknowledgments

The Helen Steiner Rice™ Foundation appreciates the cooperation of:

Baker Book House: Dwight Baker, Robin Black, Gloria Jasperse, Jeanette Thomason, Mary Wenger

Saint Francis Seraph Friary: Father James Bok, Sister Bernadette Asbach

Saint John the Baptist Province of Franciscans: Betty Karle

Pilgrim Place: Larry Bourgeois, Amy Hyatt

Sound Images, Inc.: Jack Streitmarter, Karen Rueckert, Matt Hueneman

QCA, Inc.: Cindy Johnston

Greg Ruehlmann, Dorothy Lingg, and Margie Straus for their technical assistance

Wildlife Internationalé: John and Judy Ruthven, Selma Brittingham, Kristine Riddle

Jan-Lee Music, "Let There Be Peace on Earth," © 1955, renewed 1983. All rights reserved. Used with permission.

The Benedictine Foundation of the State of Vermont, Inc., Weston Priory, Weston, Vermont, USA. Composer Weston Priory, Gregory Norbet, OSB, "Come to Me," "Peace," "Song of Hope," from recording *Locusts and Wild Honey*, © 1971. All rights reserved. Used with permission.

The Benedictine Foundation of the State of Vermont, Inc., Weston Priory, Weston, Vermont, USA. "Life Is a Journey," from recording *Move with One Heart*, © 1989. All rights reserved. Used with permission.

Joe Wise, composer, "You Fill the Day," © 1968, GIA Publications, Inc. All rights reserved. Used with permission.

Ron Harris Music, "In This Very Room," © 1979*, music by Ron Harris & Carol Harris, ASCAP. All rights reserved. Used with permission.

Maltbie B. Babcock, Terra Beata, adapted by F. L. Sheppard, "This Is My Father's World," © 1901.

Oregon Catholic Press: "On Eagle's Wings" by Michael Joncas, © 1979, New Dawn Music; and "Prayer of Saint Francis," Sebastian Temple's musical version, dedicated to Mrs. Frances Tracy, © 1967, OCP Publications, 5536 NE Hassalo, Portland, OR 97213. All rights reserved. Used with permission.

Virginia Ruehlmann Wiltse, narration

St. Ignatius Celebrate members: Jenny Sedler Bates, Mary Sedler Massa, vocal soloists; Pam Johnson Rosenacker, piano; Lisa Pollard Hasselbeck, guitar; Stacy Day, flute; Dave Gallenstein, drums; Frank Sedler, electric bass*; Lew Isaacs, drums*; and heartfelt recognition to Jenny Bates for directing the *Celebrate* group and guiding their recordings with enthusiasm and perfection

The mission of the Helen Steiner Rice™ Foundation, a nonprofit corporation, is to award grants to worthy charitable organizations that assist the elderly and needy. May peace, harmony, and tranquility increase in your life. This CD is a gift and may not be sold or reproduced.